LEONARDO DA VINCI:
Renaissance Painter

More than 500 years ago, a brilliant new age of learning and creativity dawned in Italy. The period was called the Renaissance, meaning "rebirth." During this time, many important scientists, artists and thinkers emerged in Europe. Among the greatest was Leonardo da Vinci. Nothing seemed to escape Leonardo's interest or genius.

As an artist, he painted the trace of a smile on the *Mona Lisa*. As a designer, he drew plans for magnificent castles, fantastic machines and deadly weapons. As a scientist, he was the first to sketch a baby still in its mother's womb. Leonardo was also a bold and original thinker. In his notes are rough plans for a helicopter, a parachute and even a submarine! (Remember, at Leonardo's time, warriors fought on horseback.)

What kind of man was Leonardo da Vinci? Where did his talent and creativity come from? It is a puzzle—like the mysterious smile on the *Mona Lisa*. It asks us to step into Leonardo's world of greatness.

Mason Crest
450 Parkway Drive, Suite D
Broomall, PA 19008
www.masoncrest.com

Printed and bound in the United States of America.

First printing
9 8 7 6 5 4 3 2 1

Series ISBN: 978-1-4222-2839-5
ISBN: 978-1-4222-2848-7
ebook ISBN: 978-1-4222-8968-6

The Library of Congress has cataloged the
         hardcopy format(s) as follows:

              Library of Congress Cataloging-in-Publication Data

January, Brendan, 1972-
  [Da Vinci]
  Leonardo da Vinci : Renaissance Painter / Brendan January.
     pages cm. — (People of importance)
  Previously published: Da Vinci. 2003.
  ISBN 978-1-4222-2848-7 (hardcover) — ISBN 978-1-4222-2839-5 (series) — ISBN 978-1-4222-8968-6 (ebook)
  1. Leonardo, da Vinci, 1452-1519—Juvenile literature. 2. Painters—Italy—Biography—Juvenile literature. I. Title.
  ND623.L5J36 2014
  709.2—dc23
  [B]
                              2013006217

Produced by Vestal Creative Services.
www.vestalcreative.com
Illustrations copyright © 2000 Paolo Rui

People of Importance

LEONARDO DA VINCI:

Renaissance Painter

Brendan January   Paolo Rui

Mason Crest

Leonardo was born on 15 April, 1452 in Vinci, a small town in northern Italy. Leonardo's father was a powerful lawyer. His mother was a maid. Leonardo was born out of wedlock—his parents never married. Perhaps this embarrassed Leonardo. He rarely talked about his parents for the rest of his life. Luckily, his grandfather took good care of Leonardo.

Young Leonardo grew into a strong boy who loved outdoor life. The valleys and fields around his village were filled with olive vines and chestnut trees. When his grandfather went to work in the fields, Leonardo followed. He was fascinated by the small animals and insects. Sometimes, he followed insects so closely that he strayed and got lost. But he enjoyed every moment. Any new thing gripped his attention. He would study it until he was satisfied that he knew everything about it.

Leonardo's school was the outdoors. He drew what he saw, such as newly hatched chicks emerging from their shells, the ripening wheat in fields and wild cherry trees blooming on mountain slopes. Whatever Leonardo drew—from a bird's feather to a flower—appeared to be lifelike. Even as a child, Leonardo's talent was stunning.

Leonardo's father, who spent most of his time in Florence, visited Leonardo and realised Leonardo had the talent to become a painter. Because Leonardo's mother and father were not married, Leonardo could not study to become a lawyer. Instead, thought his father, Leonardo could become an artist. When Leonardo was 14, his father took him to the city of Florence.

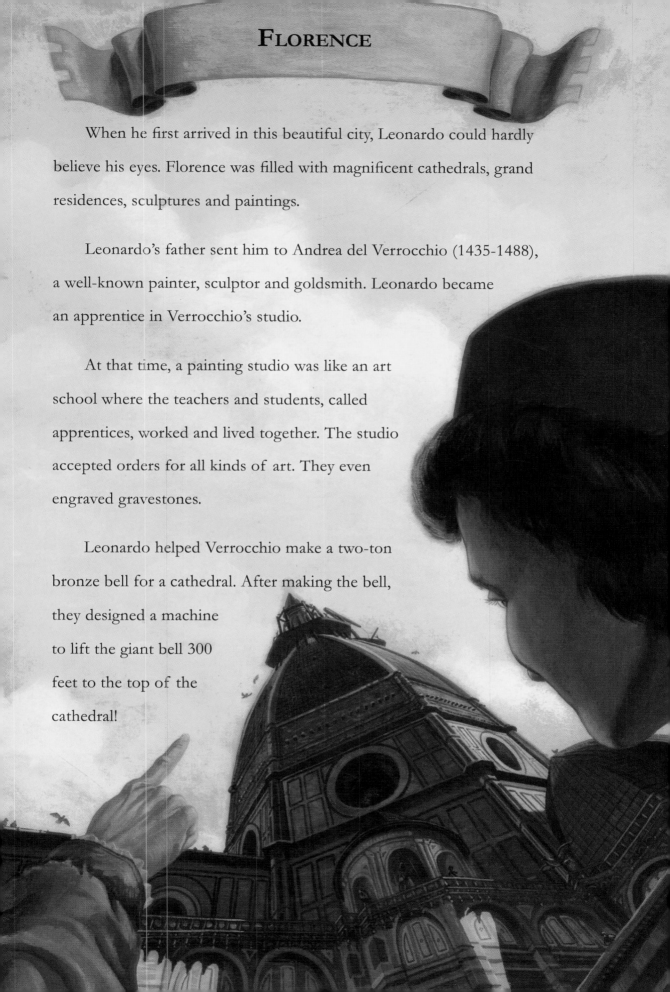

FLORENCE

When he first arrived in this beautiful city, Leonardo could hardly believe his eyes. Florence was filled with magnificent cathedrals, grand residences, sculptures and paintings.

Leonardo's father sent him to Andrea del Verrocchio (1435-1488), a well-known painter, sculptor and goldsmith. Leonardo became an apprentice in Verrocchio's studio.

At that time, a painting studio was like an art school where the teachers and students, called apprentices, worked and lived together. The studio accepted orders for all kinds of art. They even engraved gravestones.

Leonardo helped Verrocchio make a two-ton bronze bell for a cathedral. After making the bell, they designed a machine to lift the giant bell 300 feet to the top of the cathedral!

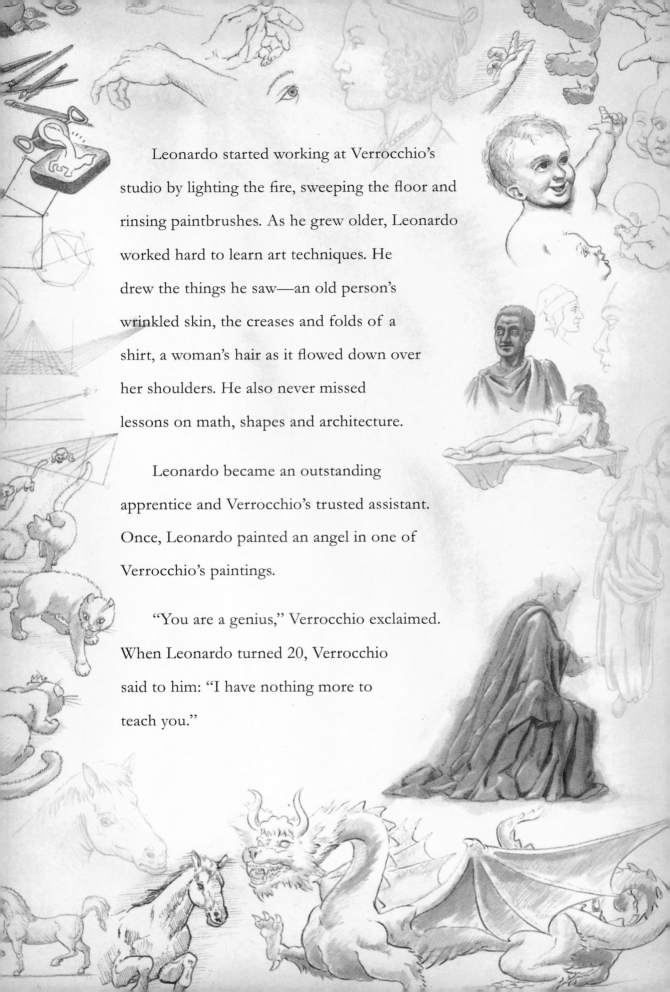

Leonardo started working at Verrocchio's studio by lighting the fire, sweeping the floor and rinsing paintbrushes. As he grew older, Leonardo worked hard to learn art techniques. He drew the things he saw—an old person's wrinkled skin, the creases and folds of a shirt, a woman's hair as it flowed down over her shoulders. He also never missed lessons on math, shapes and architecture.

Leonardo became an outstanding apprentice and Verrocchio's trusted assistant. Once, Leonardo painted an angel in one of Verrocchio's paintings.

"You are a genius," Verrocchio exclaimed. When Leonardo turned 20, Verrocchio said to him: "I have nothing more to teach you."

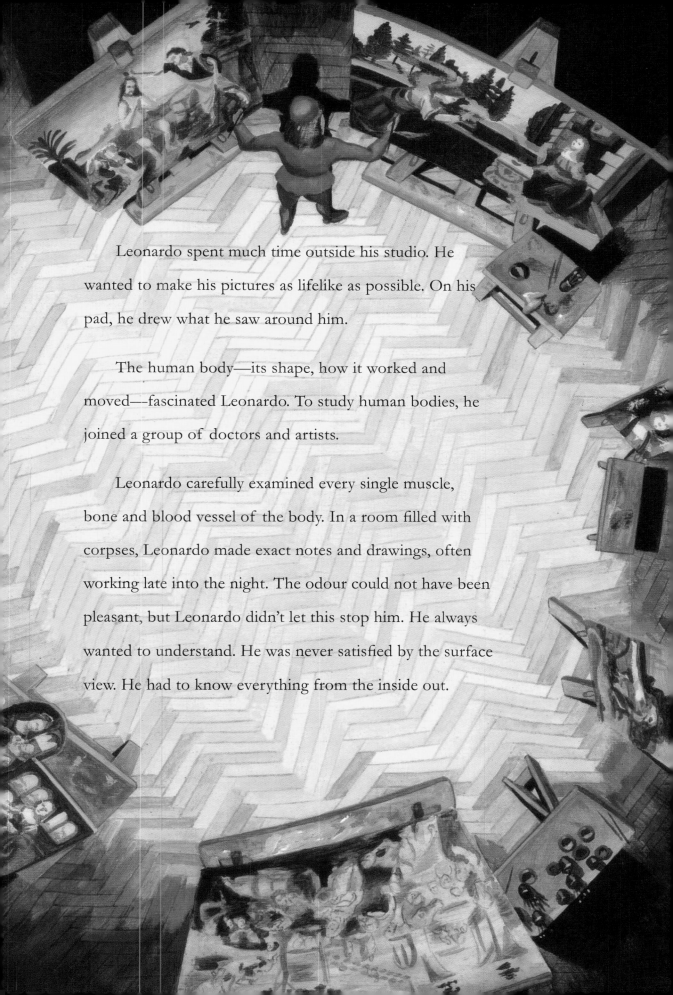

Leonardo spent much time outside his studio. He wanted to make his pictures as lifelike as possible. On his pad, he drew what he saw around him.

The human body—its shape, how it worked and moved—fascinated Leonardo. To study human bodies, he joined a group of doctors and artists.

Leonardo carefully examined every single muscle, bone and blood vessel of the body. In a room filled with corpses, Leonardo made exact notes and drawings, often working late into the night. The odour could not have been pleasant, but Leonardo didn't let this stop him. He always wanted to understand. He was never satisfied by the surface view. He had to know everything from the inside out.

TO MILAN

In 1482, at the age of 30, Leonardo left Florence for Milan, another city in northern Italy. He was eager to impress the leader of Milan, Duke Ludowic Sforza. Leonardo wrote a letter to the duke, listing ten things he could do. Leonardo explained that he was an engineer, a designer of weapons, a builder of canals, a painter and a sculptor of marble, bronze and clay.

At the end of the letter, Leonardo offered to make a statue of the duke's father. "I will do my best to make this sculpture a masterpiece that will be adored by all and remembered forever," he wrote.

The Duke of Milan was curious about such a bold young man. He invited Leonardo to his palace. "Young man, are you sure you are capable of doing so many things?" he asked. Leonardo replied with a smile, "Many things I could do were not listed in the letter."

The duke offered him work, and Leonardo left Florence.

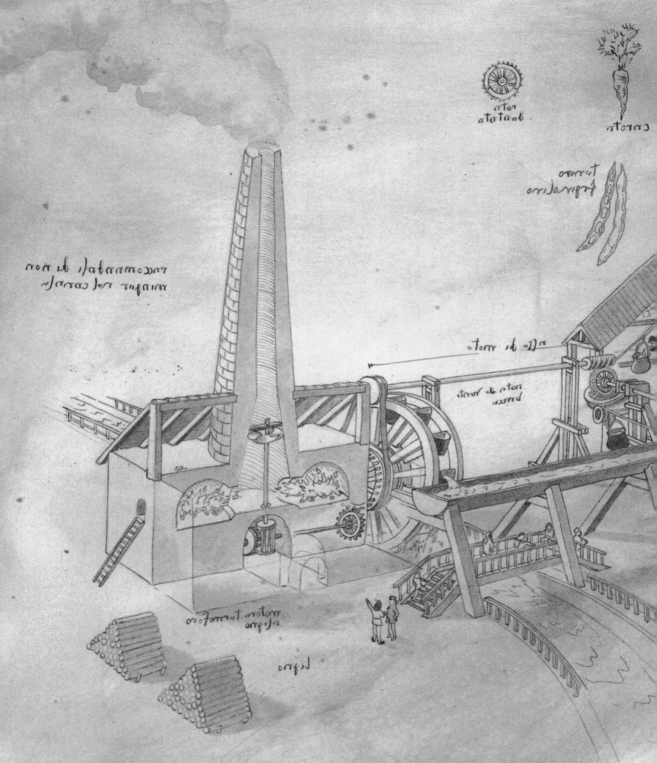

Leonardo opened a studio in Milan and began teaching apprentices. He also read a great deal and performed experiments. His observations and ideas were written down in notebooks. Few things escaped Leonardo's interest. On a single page, he sketched bird feathers and plans for a clock. In the corners were mathematical formulas hastily jotted down.

Leonardo wrote his words backward. To read his notes today, you have to hold them up to a mirror. Some say he wanted to keep his ideas secret. After Leonardo arrived in Milan, a church asked him to paint a picture called *The Virgin of the Rocks.*

The Milanese flocked to Leonardo's studio and gasped at the painting's beauty. But the group that asked for the painting said it didn't contain the correct number of people. They even accused Leonardo of cheating. Leonardo, however, wouldn't change his painting. He thought that a true artist must complete a work according to his own idea.

The Milan duke wanted to expand the size of his city and his power, and he often battled his neighbours. He urged Leonardo to build him new weapons. Leonardo hated war. "War is nothing but the behavior of crazed animals," he once said. Still, Leonardo obeyed the duke. His notebooks from this period are filled with sketches of contraptions and weapons. One drawing looks like a machine gun and a tank combined. Leonardo even planned a flying machine to carry soldiers! The Duke of Milan next asked Leonardo to make a statue of his father riding on a horse. Even better, Leonardo could finish the sculpture as he saw fit.

Leonardo eagerly went to work. He filled sketchbooks with drawings of horses prancing, snorting, running, jumping. Using clay, he fashioned a full-size model.

Leonardo planned to cast the largest bronze monument in history. His ideas were so advanced that the machinery to build such a statue didn't yet exist. The bronze was gathered for the statue, but in the 1490s, war broke out between Milan and France. The bronze was taken to make cannons.

Later, French archers used Leonardo's clay model for target practice, shattering it. To this day, people have wondered: Could Leonardo have made his grand statue?

DVODECEDRON ELEVA
TVS VACVS

In 1495, the Duke of Milan asked Leonardo to paint a mural for a monastery. The scene was from the Bible—the Last Supper, in which Jesus shared a final meal with his closest followers.

Delighted with this subject, Leonardo went many places for inspiration. He went to taverns to watch people drink and eat. He sketched their faces and how they sat. Later, many of these images would appear in *The Last Supper*. As Leonardo worked on the painting, the abbot, leader of the monastery, would stop and watch. He even made some suggestions, which annoyed Leonardo greatly. The abbot complained to the Duke that Leonardo often stared at the wall for long moments without painting a stroke.

Leonardo responded to the Duke that he was searching for a face for Judas, the betrayer. Perhaps, Leonardo suggested, the abbot's face would be the best choice.

The Last Supper is Leonardo's most beautiful work in Milan. The painting is unlike any before it. At that time, paintings were supposed to tell a story. But Leonardo focuses on one moment. Every figure is lifelike. Through the expressions and poses of the disciples, Leonardo showed their fear, suspicion and anger.

Unfortunately, Leonardo used a new kind of paint for the picture. It didn't work. After only two years, the paint started to peel.

Human postures and movements reflect the fluctuation of their thoughts.

—Leonardo da Vinci

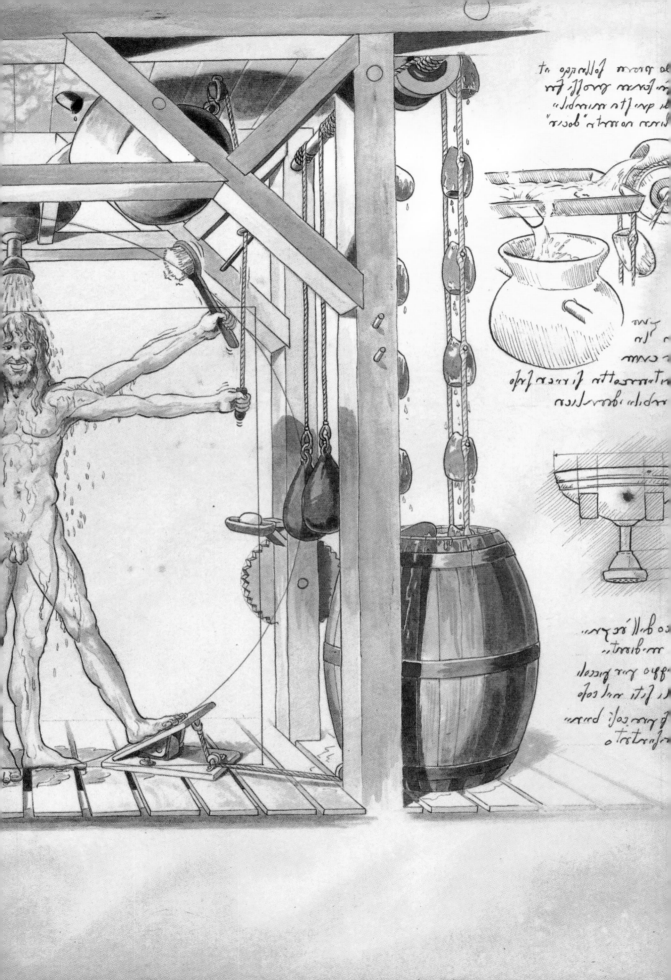

Leonardo created many of his works for the church, and he knew many priests. One, named Lucas Pacioli, wrote a book on math and geometry that inspired Leonardo. Leonardo became Pacioli's student. Geometry, which measures space, helped Leonardo make calculations in his paintings and sculpture. Pacioli and Leonardo published a book together called *On Divine Proportion*. Pacioli wrote the numbers and formulas, while Leonardo used his brilliant pen and paintbrush to portray geometric designs.

Leonardo once said that art is science. A painting should be like a mirror to the outside world. But Leonardo also said that the painter should not just copy nature.

Leonardo spent most his time studying the world and creating art. He never married.

In 1499, Milan and France again went to war, and French soldiers captured the city. Leonardo was forced to leave his home of 17 years and seek work elsewhere. He visited the Italian city of Mantua, where he planned a portrait for Marchioness Isabella d'Este. But he left quickly, leaving only a pencil drawing behind.

He also travelled to the lagoon city of Venice, where he studied waterways. Venice is a maze of canals, and most of the residents move around on boats. Leonardo was inspired by the movements of fish. He concluded that adding a few more oars to a boat would greatly increase its speed.

About this time, Leonardo's notes fill with designs for a submarine, snorkels and diving suits. Even when travelling in a strange city, Leonardo never stopped imagining. But Leonardo was also always interested in something new. He rarely finished any work, something that has puzzled people for centuries.

In 1500, Leonardo returned to Florence after an absence of 18 years. But even Florence was threatened by the warfare that was sweeping through Italy. Leonardo was hired to create weapons for the army. Leonardo marched with the troops, filling pages with notes. He drew maps of their routes and studied new weapons—scaling ladders and portable bridges, castles with secret supply routes.

When the army was attacking the city of Pisa, Leonardo thought of a new strategy. The Pisan defenders relied on the River Arno for food and weapons. Leonardo suggested that they divert the river from the city, cutting Pisa off. The project was begun but kept collapsing. Finally, it was abandoned.

Perhaps because Leonardo detested war, he gave up military projects and returned to Florence. There, he began painting the *Mona Lisa*. The *Mona Lisa* is the most well-known portrait in the world. Countless numbers of painters have tried to copy it. Countless others have tried to understand the emotion behind Mona Lisa's faint smile.

Who was Mona Lisa? How did Leonardo paint such a mysterious and beautiful woman?

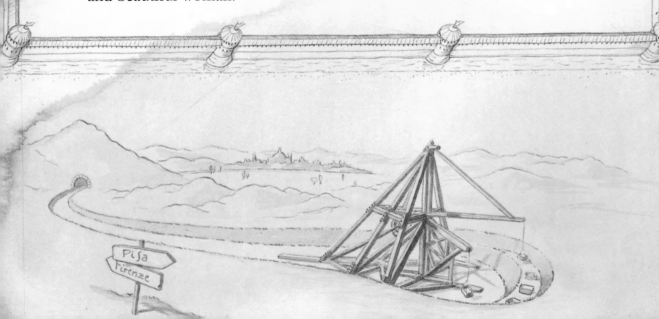

Some say Mona Lisa was the wife of Francesco del Giocondo, a banker. Others have used computers to study the painting. What did they find out? They said the painting is a self-portrait of Leonardo himself!

No matter who Mona Lisa was, it must have been difficult for her to sit still for such a long time until the painting was completed. Leonardo may have brought musicians and comedians to perform and keep her in a good mood.

By the time Leonardo finished *Mona Lisa*, younger artists, such as Raphael Sanzio and Michelangelo Buonarroti, were becoming famous.

In 1504, Leonardo was asked to paint a scene of the Battle of Anghiari in Florence's city hall. Michelangelo was also asked to paint another battle scene for the opposite wall. The true battle did not occur in the paintings, but between the painters. Both Leonardo and Michelangelo did their best to create earthshaking scenes. Hundreds of drafts were produced. The two criticised each other's designs and paints. They went so far as to insult each other's clothing and talent.

The battle between the two painters came to an unexpected end. Michelangelo went to serve the Pope in Rome shortly after finishing his first draft. Leonardo painted his scene, but he committed another disastrous error by trying new paints. The paint ran down the work before it was even finished. The two painters never finished. To this day, people wonder what the paintings would have looked like.

What more could he do? As he grew older, Leonardo put down his paintbrush and recalled a dream of his youth: flight. He turned his attention to birds and sketched them in flight, gathering food and playing with each other. He made careful notes of their bodies and wings.

At night, Leonardo watched bats circle in the dark sky. From these observations, Leonardo made designs that are similar to today's parachutes and glider wings.

Without today's technology, Leonardo could never turn his dreams into reality. He nevertheless used his imagination to soar.

Whenever Leonardo da Vinci passed a place where birds were sold he would buy the birds and then open their cages and let them return to the skies.

—Giorgio Vasari, artist and biographer

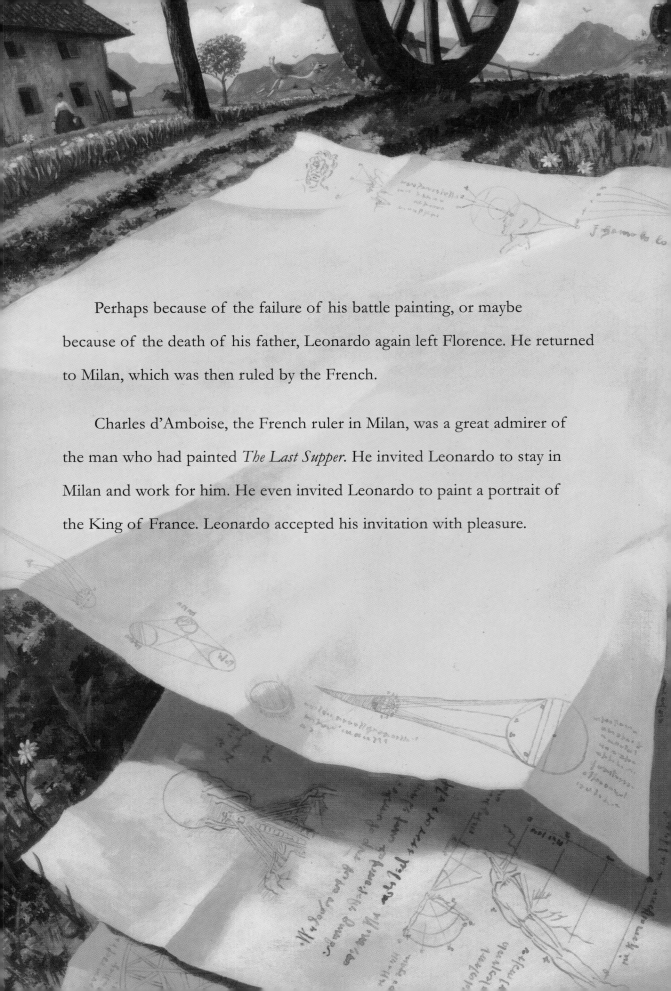

Perhaps because of the failure of his battle painting, or maybe because of the death of his father, Leonardo again left Florence. He returned to Milan, which was then ruled by the French.

Charles d'Amboise, the French ruler in Milan, was a great admirer of the man who had painted *The Last Supper*. He invited Leonardo to stay in Milan and work for him. He even invited Leonardo to paint a portrait of the King of France. Leonardo accepted his invitation with pleasure.

During this period, Leonardo was free to study the body or spend time organising his enormous collection of notes. He also completed another painting, *The Virgin and Child with St. Anne.*

After *The Virgin and Child with St. Anne,* Leonardo rarely painted again. He devoted his time to his scientific studies.

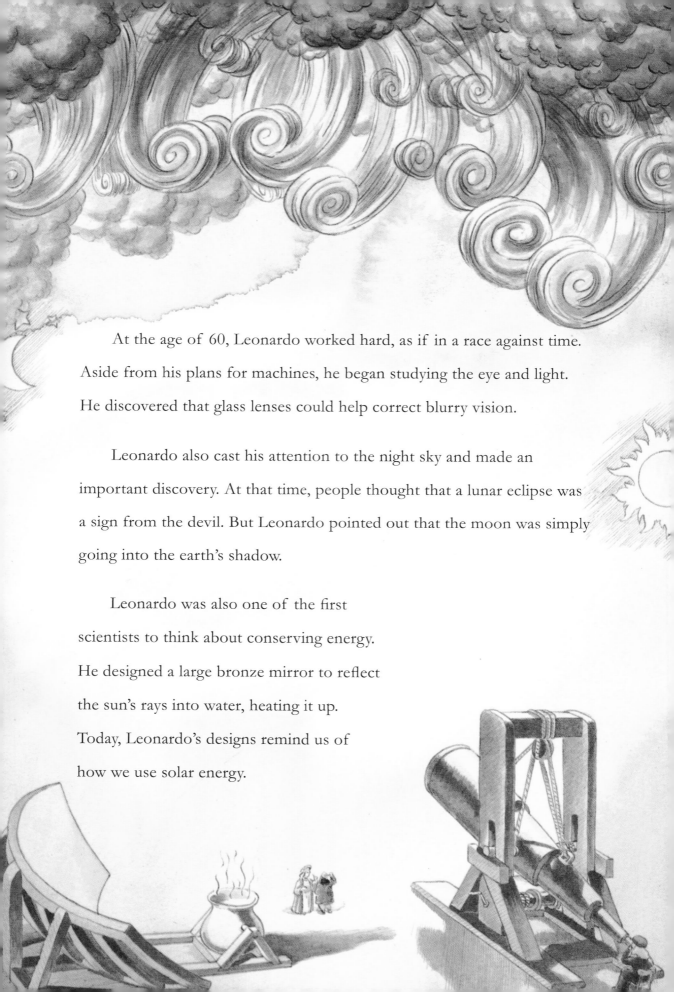

At the age of 60, Leonardo worked hard, as if in a race against time. Aside from his plans for machines, he began studying the eye and light. He discovered that glass lenses could help correct blurry vision.

Leonardo also cast his attention to the night sky and made an important discovery. At that time, people thought that a lunar eclipse was a sign from the devil. But Leonardo pointed out that the moon was simply going into the earth's shadow.

Leonardo was also one of the first scientists to think about conserving energy. He designed a large bronze mirror to reflect the sun's rays into water, heating it up. Today, Leonardo's designs remind us of how we use solar energy.

FRANCE'S GLORY

In 1516, the new king of France, Francis I, invited Leonardo to visit him as guest. Leonardo accepted and brought his notes, paintings and an apprentice to France.

But Leonardo's health was failing. His eyes were growing dim, and his right hand was disabled. Nevertheless, Francis I heaped honours on Leonardo. Leonardo was given a castle on the king's grounds, and a road was built between the king's castle and Leonardo's so the king could get Leonardo's advice at any time.

Though Leonardo's body grew weak and frail, his mind refused to halt. "I shall continue to work," he wrote in his notes. His last great project was the design for a gigantic new castle for Francis I, to be built on the banks of the Loire River.

Leonardo designed the castle to be both a grand home and a fort to protect France. The ancient city of Rome, Italy, was his blueprint.

Within the castle, Leonardo designed a new drainage system, bridges, a garden and an automatic sprinkling fountain.

He made a model of the castle for the king. Regrettably, Leonardo suffered a stroke soon afterward, and his dream castle was never built. On 2 May, 1519, Leonardo left our world. But has he really left us?

Aren't his paintings and notes carefully preserved in major art galleries around the world? Haven't many people tried to fulfill the dreams he left in his drafts? Haven't the people of Milan finally built the bronze statue of the father of the Duke of Milan?

Isn't Mona Lisa's smile still with us?

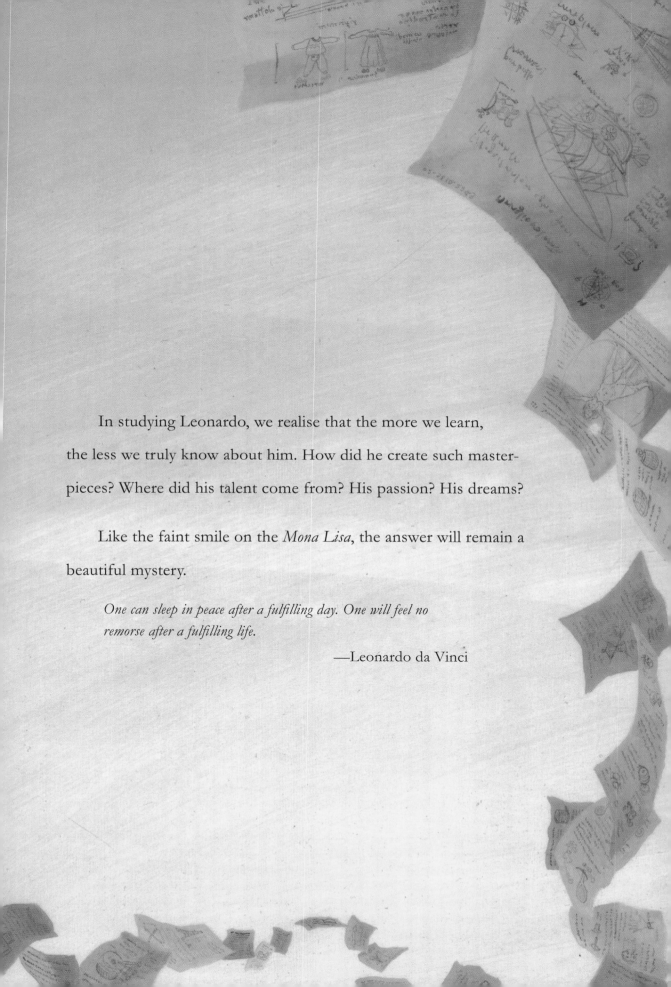

In studying Leonardo, we realise that the more we learn,
the less we truly know about him. How did he create such master-
pieces? Where did his talent come from? His passion? His dreams?

Like the faint smile on the *Mona Lisa*, the answer will remain a
beautiful mystery.

*One can sleep in peace after a fulfilling day. One will feel no
remorse after a fulfilling life.*

—Leonardo da Vinci

LEONARDO DA VINCI ART GALLERY

1 Baptism of Christ

Leonardo's earliest known painting is an angel in the *Baptism of Christ*, which he completed with Verrocchio. He painted the small angel at the lower left of the painting. The angel's back is to the viewer. Painted with soft lines and a gentle smile, the angel watches the baptism of Jesus Christ with awe. Young Leonardo captured the angel's spirit of devotion.

2, 3, 4, 5 Portrait of Ginevra de'Benci, Madonna with the Carnation, The Annunciation, The Adoration of the Magi

Leonardo completed several paintings in Florence, including the *Portrait of Ginevra de' Benci; The Annunciation; The Adoration of the Magi;* and the *Madonna with the Carnation*. He never finished *The Adoration of the Magi*, which was supposed to contain many figures.

Leonardo experimented with different painting techniques. In *The Annunciation*, he used an oil painting technique used in northern Italy. Since oil paint took so long to dry, he could blend different colours to show the contrast between shadow and light. This technique became common in paintings of the Renaissance.

6 The Virgin of the Rocks

In this painting, the figures are arranged in a giant triangle, a symbol of stability. The Virgin Mary is the centre of the painting. On her left stands an angel and the boy John. On her right is the baby Jesus. Leonardo painted a deep brown in the background, to give the painting a mood of warmth and mystery. The painting shows Leonardo's skill. The faces, hands, mountains and plants are all painted realistically.

4

5

7 The Last Supper

The Last Supper is one of the most powerful scenes in the Bible. It portrays Jesus gathered together with his 12 disciples. Leonardo's painting captures the moment when Jesus declares, "One of you will betray me." Look closely at how Leonardo has painted the disciples' reaction to Jesus' words. Some are shocked. Some protest. Some gesture in disbelief. Leonardo has captured their complex emotions and created a masterpiece. Unfortunately, *The Last Supper* has been damaged by time. When mixing the paints, Leonardo tried a new approach. The result was a disaster. Even before Leonardo died, the paint started peeling and the bright colours fading.

8 The Human Body

Leonardo has written that each body can be precisely measured. For example, the length of your arms stretched out from fingertip to fingertip equals your height.

9 Mona Lisa

Leonardo used a special method to paint the *Mona Lisa*. He heated the paints so the brush strokes melted away, leaving a hazy, mysterious look. Viewers have been fascinated by the *Mona Lisa* for hundreds of years. Look at her closely. Is she smiling or not?

10 The Virgin and Child with St. Anne

This is a painting of family love. The Virgin Mary sits in the lap of her mother, St. Anne. The child Jesus plays at their side. St. Anne gazes down at her daughter, while Mary smiles at Jesus and reaches out to hold him. Jesus wrestles with a lamb, a symbol of peace and sacrifice.

8

9

10

BIOGRAPHY

Brendan January was born and raised in Pleasantville, New York. After graduating from Haverford College in 1995, January earned his master's degree from Columbia Graduate School of Journalism. January is an award-winning writer of juvenile nonfiction and is currently a journalist at the *Philadelphia Inquirer*. He lives with his wife in New Jersey.